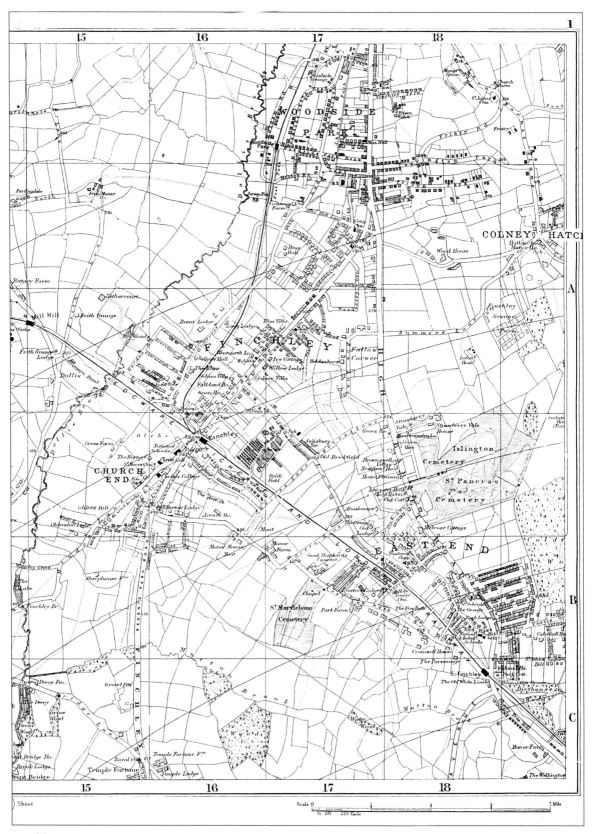

Finchley in 1914.

FINCHLEY

PAST & PRESENT

East End Lane, *c.* 1900.

IN OLD PHOTOGRAPHS

BRITAIN

FINCHLEY

PAST & PRESENT

CLIVE & DAVID SMITH

SUTTON PUBLISHING

Sutton Publishing Limited
Phoenix Mill · Thrupp · Stroud
Gloucestershire · GL5 2BU

First published 2003

Copyright © Clive & David Smith, 2003

Half Title page: Summers Lane, *c.* 1900.
Title page: Express Dairy cart, *c.* 1905.
Front endpaper: Woodhouse Corner, *c.* 1925.
Back endpaper: Woodhouse Corner, 2002.

British Library Cataloguing in Publication Data
A catalogue record for this book is available from the British Library.

ISBN 0-7509-2916-2

Typeset in 10.5/13.5 Photina.
Typesetting and origination by
Sutton Publishing Limited.
Printed and bound in England by
J.H. Haynes & Co. Ltd, Sparkford.

Baker's cart, *c.* 1905.

CONTENTS

Nether Street, *c.* 1905.

H. Dowdall, builder and decorator, 6a High Street, North Finchley, *c.* 1905.

INTRODUCTION

The ancient spelling of Finchley was Fyncheslee, or Findelee-leya, possibly derived from finch (meaning bird) and the Old English leah (a forest) – meaning the clearing in the forest with finches. Another explanation, probably more likely, is that it is derived from a personal name such as Finch – meaning Finch's Forest. Finchley is not mentioned in the Domesday Book (1086). This is probably because it was part of the Bishop of London's lands and not shown separately.

Finchley Common was once estimated to contain 2,000 acres. It was frequently used in olden times for military encampments. In February 1660 General Monk drew up his army here on his famous march to London, just before the restoration of Charles II. When the Pretender invaded England in 1745 a camp was formed here, and the disorderly march of the Guards to it gave rise to Hogarth's well-known picture, *The March to Finchley*. In the eighteenth century it formed the happy hunting-ground of highwaymen and footpads. At the London end of the common, near the junction of Oak Road and High Road, East Finchley, stood an old oak tree known as Turpin's Oak, where it was believed that Dick Turpin often took his stand; and the infamous Jack Sheppard finally had his career cut short here, being captured near the common in 1724.

There are several reports of prize-fights taking place on Finchley Common. This fight was reported in the London *Daily Chronicle* in 1787:

> This day a great boxing match was fought in Finchley Common between Mendoza, a Jew, and one Marrin a butcher from Bath, on which bets to great amount depended. After about half an hour's fine boxing the match was decided in favour of Mendoza. There were many thousand spectators and among them some of the first personages of the Kingdom.

Highwaymen in Finchley

Finchley Common in the eighteenth and nineteenth centuries was one of the most dangerous places in the country because of the activities of highwaymen and footpads. The size and wildness of the common was so great that it became a popular haunt for these criminals. In fiction these villains are often portrayed in a romantic manner, but the truth about these men is that they were more often than not callous and savage murderers. This report from the *Gentleman's Magazine* of 1699 records a particularly savage attack:

> On July 11th, Mr Robert Leader and his servant were travelling from London across Finchley Common. They were attacked by Edmund Tooll, known as 'Tooley'. Tooll and

Hendon Lane, 1870.

his companions knocked Leader from his horse and brutally stamped on his face and stomach, until he begged for his life. They then let him rise and as he turned his back to walk away Tooll shot him in the back wounding him so seriously that he died the next day. Tooll was arrested in Jermyn Street, London, he resisted, firing at the police and attempting to stab one of the constables with a short sword. Even in the court he continued to be aggressive, saying he wished that he had stabbed the policeman in the heart. He was executed on 2 February 1700 and afterwards his body was put in chains and displayed on Finchley Common. It was normal practice to exhibit the body on a gibbet as a deterrent to other criminals. There were a number of these gibbets, one almost opposite the Bald Faced Stag and another at the Tally Ho corner.

In 1816 the common stretched north to south from Totteridge Lane to the present day East Finchley station, and east to west from Muswell Hill to Dollis Brook. Finchley was noted for its very large Hog Market, situated at the hamlet of East End until the 1860s. Said to be the first in the country, it was held

Ye Olde King of Prussia, *c.* 1900.

in the open space in front of the George public house. This market is mentioned in E.W. Brayley's *Beauties of England and Wales* (1810): 'Hogs are kept in considerable numbers. They are brought from Shropshire and other distant counties, and sold at a large market on Finchley Common'.

By the middle of the nineteenth century the common, as a large area of waste land, was no more. Much of the land was enclosed and some 90 acres were taken to form the cemetery for St Pancras and Islington in 1854. The St Marylebone Cemetery dates from 1855. The hamlet of North End (North Finchley) grew up on Finchley Common, and Christ Church was erected here in 1870.

In 1859 Hendon Lane was known as Finchley Hill, and ran from Hendon to Church End, Finchley. Around this time the common was gradually put to grass. In turn small dairies grew up, serving an area of about 5 miles each, although the most important crop was hay for the ever-expanding horse population of London. At this time hay and water were as important as petrol is today. Most of the ordinary people living in Finchley would have been agricultural labourers earning a meagre living.

The coming of the railways was to have a significant effect on the development of Finchley, the population rising from 4,937 in 1861 to 11,191 by 1881. The Great Northern Railway Company opened a branch line from Highgate to Edgware on 22 August 1867. The station at Church End was known as Finchley and Hendon until it became Finchley, Church End, on 1 February 1894. It was renamed Finchley Central on 1 April 1940. London Transport (Underground) trains began using it on 14 April 1940. Woodside Park station opened as 'Torrington Park Woodside' on 1 April 1872; it was renamed Woodside Park on 1 May 1882. London Transport Underground Northern Line trains began using this station on 14 April 1940.

Avenue House, *c.* 1920.

East Finchley station opened as East End Finchley on 1 December 1867 and was renamed East Finchley on 1 February 1887. This station was reconstructed with a two-island platform in 1939. London Transport's Northern Line began using East Finchley station on 3 July 1939. West Finchley Station opened on 1 March 1933. London Transport Underground trains started using this station on 14 April 1940.

Finchley Church, dedicated, like the neighbouring parish churches of Hendon and Harrow, to St Mary, stands high, its short square tower well backed by trees. While the origins of the church are much earlier it dates basically from the fifteenth century. The church was thoroughly restored in 1872, when about £4,000 was spent in restorations and additions, the stonework being allowed to emerge from the heavy coatings of plaster with which it had long been covered. The building was severely damaged by a 1,000lb German bomb during an air raid on 4 October 1940; restoration was not completed until 1953.

Finchley, Middlesex grew from being a pleasant rural village, 8 miles north of London to a considerable district lying between Hampstead and Highgate in the south and Whetstone and Barnet in the north. The population was 7,146 in 1871. James Thorne, writing in 1876, described it thus:

The village (Church End) is long, rambling, still rural, and not unpicturesque, the country lanes and road changing imperceptibly into the village street; everywhere trees mingling with the houses, and the village culminating in a striking group of buildings

– the church the centre, the old part of Finchley College on one side, the new building with its tall tower on the other. But the builder is steadily gaining ground here as elsewhere. Streets, terraces, villas and cottages are rising all around and the outlying hamlets thereafter soon to become good-sized villages. There is a little inn with a quaint garden, 'The King of Prussia' at Church End.

The early years of the twentieth century marked the end of a more leisurely age and the beginning of a newer brisker era. The population in 1901 was 22,126 and by 1911 it had risen to 39,419. Thousands of houses were built, almost 400 a year, between 1904 and 1914. The grass verges and hedges which lined the roads disappeared and the horse drawn buses began to be replaced by the motor-bus and electric tram.

'Lord' George Sanger.

Henry Charles Stephens.

Finchley Carnival has been in existence for a hundred years. It was started in 1902 by local businessmen to enhance the area and raise money for charity. One of the earliest recipients of this was the Finchley Cottage Hospital. 'Lord' George Sanger, the circus promoter, was a great supporter of the Carnival. In the early years he provided some of his circus animals for the parade. Sanger lived at Park Farm from 1904 until 1911 when he was murdered by one of his employees.

In 1873 Henry Charles Stephens acquired Avenue House. He was the son of Dr Henry Stephens, who invented fluid ink. During the First World War the house was used as a hospital for Flying Corps pilots. In 1927 the house and grounds were assigned to Finchley Urban District Council by Stephens' executors. He had stated in his will that the house and grounds should always be open to the public. It

Margaret Thatcher at College Farm.

was at Avenue House on 5 October 1933 that the Earl of Athlone presented Finchley with its charter incorporating it as a borough. In September 2002 Barnet Council agreed to grant a 125-year lease to the Avenue House Management Committee. The estate will now be run by an eleven-member committee who will run the estate as a charitable trust.

The first bombs to fall on Finchley during the Second World War were five small high explosive bombs that landed on the Sewage Disposal Works on the night of 27 August 1940. No one was hurt and only superficial damage was caused. The last bomb in Finchley was a long-range rocket (V-2) which fell at Abbots Gardens on 15 November 1944. Four people were killed and forty injured, and there was considerable damage to property. From first to last Finchley received 213 high explosive bombs, 126 groups of incendiary bombs, 14 oil bombs, 4 parachute mines, 7 flying bombs and 1 long-range rocket. In addition 39 unexploded bombs and 1 unexploded parachute mine were dealt with. Seventy-eight people were killed and 336 injured. Many houses were destroyed and a great many more damaged.

The Metropolitan borough of Finchley was amalgamated, on 1 April 1965, with the urban districts of Barnet, East Barnet, Friern Barnet and the Borough of Hendon to form the London Borough of Barnet, one of the largest boroughs in London.

Margaret Thatcher was elected Member of Parliament for Finchley in 1959. She became leader of the Conservative Party in 1975. In the 1979 general election she led the party to victory and became Britain's first female prime minister. She held the position for eleven and a half years and won three general elections.

1
Church End

Hendon Lane and Christ's College, *c.* 1875. The pond situated at the corner of Hendon Lane and Gravel Hill was filled in in 1885.

Hendon Lane, *c.* 1900. This rural view looking towards Finchley shows the bridge over the waterfall and brook. *Below:* a slightly more animated view today with the junction of the A1.

Regents Park Road, *c*. 1910. Mountfield Road is on the right. The man riding his bicycle towards Church End has the road to himself apart from a solitary tramcar! *Below*: a modern bus follows the same route.

La Delivrance statue, *c.* 1935. Situated near the junction of Regents Park Road and the North Circular Road, the statue was inspired by the Allied victory at the Battle of the Marne and designed by M. Guillaume. It was presented to Finchley by Lord Rothermere in 1926. *Below*: the road is being swept in 2002.

College Farm, *c*. 1950. Some time before 1880 the Express Dairy Company acquired about 200 acres of land (Sheephouse Farm) off Regents Park Road, and began to build a model dairy. In 1883 the buildings were completed and College Farm became a showplace of all that was best in livestock and equipment. A household delivery service was soon in operation. *Below*: College Farm as it is today. Express Dairy moved out in 1972; since then the farm has survived as an educational resource, run by the College Farm Trust. The trust is at present negotiating to buy the buildings and 10 acres of the land from the Ministry of Transport. The farm was closed in February 2001 because of the foot and mouth epidemic. All the farm animals were sold in September 2001. There is a pet food shop and a saddlery selling riding equipment and country clothing.

Allandale Avenue, looking towards Regents Park Road, *c.* 1930. The land on the left is College Farm. *Right*: the view across to Regents Park Road, *c.* 1930. *Below*: the scene today.

Beechwood Avenue, *c*. 1920 and today. This picture was taken from near the junction with Regents Park Road. Car parking was clearly not a problem then.

Holly Park, *c.* 1914. Orchard Avenue is on the right. *Below*: the tree in the road has not survived.

Manor Parade, Regents Park Road, at the crossroads with Gravel Hill and East End Road, *c.* 1920 and today.

Regents Park Road looking towards Ballards Lane, with Gravel Hill on the left and the Queen's Head public house on the right, *c.* 1914. This building dates from 1868. *Below*: the busy junction as it is today.

Gravel Hill, looking towards Regents Park Road *c*. 1910. This tranquil view, with not a vehicle in sight, contrasts with the modern view below.

Hendon Lane near the junction with Rawlins Close, *c.* 1920. *Below*: the view today shows that some of the houses have been demolished and replaced by blocks of flats.

Elm Park Road, looking towards Nether Street, *c.* 1910. *Below*: the more familiar view with parked cars on both sides. The road is much quieter since the closure of Gordon Road, which stopped it being used as a short cut.

St Mary's Avenue showing the unusual design of the Turret, *c.* 1905. Today the Turret is obscured by the trees. *Inset*: proof that it is still there in 2002.

Hendon Lane, near the junction with St Mary's Avenue, *c.* 1908. The tower of the Christ's College building can be seen. *Below*: this is the scene today with a single-decker bus on its way to Brent Cross shopping centre.

Hendon Lane showing Christ's College, *c.* 1930. The building, which dates from 1860, was built to the designs of Anthony Salvin. Christ's College was founded in 1857 by the Revd Thomas Reader White, Rector of Finchley. This distinctive building is now occupied by Pardes House Grammar School. Christ's College School is now in East End Road.

Hendon Lane, *c.* 1905. The Finchley fire brigade is seen outside the old Finchley Fire Station. The engine on the left was one of the first motor-powered fire engines to be used by a public brigade. It was delivered to the Finchley brigade on 23 November 1904 by Merryweather & Sons of Greenwich. *Below*: remarkably, all the buildings have survived.

Hendon Lane, *c.* 1908. The 'manual' fire engine was made ready for the Carnival and is seen outside St Mary's church. *Below*: St Mary's church today, with a wall replacing the hedge.

Municipal Offices (Urban District Council Offices), *c.* 1930. This building was originally a public house called the Queen's Head. The offices were destroyed by enemy bombing on 4 October 1940. *Below*: today the library stands in the place of the municipal offices.

A leisurely scene showing Victoria Parade, Hendon Lane, *c.* 1910. A horse-drawn delivery cart is being unloaded at the kerb, contrasting markedly with the current scene below.

Hendon Lane from the junction with Regents Park Road, *c.* 1900. Clement's nursery is in the centre of the picture with Christ's College towering above.

St Mary's school,
Hendon Lane, near
the junction with
Victoria Avenue,
c. 1923. The school
moved to a new
building in Dollis
Park in 1990. The
old school buildings
were demolished and
replaced by Barnet
County Court, as
seen below. *Right*: the
whole school
assembled to
celebrate Empire Day.

Regents Park Road, *c*. 1905. A typical Edwardian street scene, showing a horse bus and horse drawn carts going about their business. *Inset*: the original Finchley Conservative Association building, *c*. 1887. *Below*: the view today, contrasting sharply with the older photographs.

Regents Park Road, *c.* 1935. On the right the New Bohemia cinema, opened in 1920, was designed by C. Dudley Lewis. It closed on 4 April 1959. *Inset*: the New Bohemia, and right, an advertisement for the cinema.

Lichfield Grove, *c.* 1910. This image shows the view towards Regents Park Road. Some of the older houses have been replaced by newer ones in the current picture below.

Station Road, looking towards Wooton Grove on the right, *c.* 1910. The left-hand side was open land but is now occupied by a mixture of residential and commercial buildings, as seen below.

Sylvan Avenue from Lichfield Grove, *c.* 1914. The sports ground is at the end of the road. *Below*: Sylvan Avenue today – pavements, cars and more street furniture.

Regents Park Road looking toward Ballards Lane, *c.* 1919. On the left is the Old King of Prussia. *Right*: Ye Olde King of Prussia, *c.* 1895. *Below*: the modern development on the left was built in 1965 and there is a modern bar called the Dignity on the site.

Ballards Lane at the junction with Nether Street, *c.* 1914. On the corner on the left is the Railway Hotel. It was built in 1869 and demolished in 1962. *Below*: today Central House towers above the scene, and there is a bar called the Central on the ground floor.

Ballards Lane looking towards Hendon Lane with Station Road on the left, *c.* 1910. *Below*: today, the old bank building is occupied by solicitors.

The railway station, then known as Church End station, *c.* 1908. The arrival of the railways in the 1860s was to have a significant effect on the population and development of Finchley. The population rose from 4,937 in 1861 to 11,191 in 1881.

Finchley Church End. This station was opened by the Great Northern Railway as Finchley and Hendon on 22 August 1867; it became Finchley (Church End) on 1 February 1894 and Finchley Central on 1 April 1940. It was first used by the London Underground in April 1940. *Below*: a High Barnet tube train arriving at the station.

2

Ballards Lane

Ballards Lane, near Redbourne Avenue, with St Margaret's United
Reform Church on the right, *c.* 1904.

Ballards Lane looking towards Hendon Lane and showing Popes garage on the right, *c.* 1930. *Below:* the Victorian shops have gone, to be replaced by late twentieth-century development, including a large Tesco store to serve the needs of a modern London suburb.

Redbourne Avenue from Ballards Lane, *c.* 1905. On the right is St Margaret's United Reform Church. *Below*: today the church has been demolished and replaced by a Barclays Bank building.

Ballards Lane looking towards North Finchley, *c.* 1925 and today. A leisurely scene near the junction with Redbourne Avenue. St Margaret's Church is on the right behind the trees.

Dollis Road, *c.* 1908. These crossroads show Crescent Road on the left and Nether Street on the right. The unmade road and lack of vehicles contrast with the view almost a century later. *Inset*: Nether Street crossroads, *c.* 1930.

Ballards Lane looking north, *c.* 1925.
On the left is the Express Dairy shop on
the corner of the Grove. *Inset*: Parke's
Drug Stores, now a fried chicken outlet.
Below: Ballards Lane, 2002.

Ballards Lane, *c*. 1930. On the left can be seen the Joiners Arms public house.

Ballards Lane, *c.* 1907. The buildings are familiar, even if the clothes and traffic belong to another age. Three horses are pulling the bus towards Hendon, but these were soon to be replaced by the tram. *Below*: today a single-decker no. 143 bus is en route to Brent Cross shopping centre.

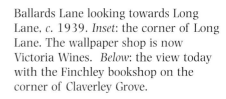

Ballards Lane looking towards Long Lane, *c.* 1939. *Inset*: the corner of Long Lane. The wallpaper shop is now Victoria Wines. *Below*: the view today with the Finchley bookshop on the corner of Claverley Grove.

Long Lane, *c.* 1930. This photograph was taken from the corner of Dukes Avenue with the Victoria Recreation Ground on the right.

Finchley Fire Station, Long Lane, was opened in December 1935 at the junction with the North Circular Road. Recent improvements have removed the junction and replaced it with a flyover. *Below*: the fire station remains today.

Ballards Lane looking towards Wentworth Park on the right, *c.* 1940. *Below*: the Welcome Café is still going and there is a motor dealer in the same building as before.

Ballards Lane Police Station, *c.* 1910. In 1886 there was reported a need for a sub-divisional station to be built at Finchley. A new site called Wentworth Lodge was found and when the asking price of £2,700 was reduced to £2,400 it and the 1¼ acre piece of land were purchased by the Home Office. This station was closed in 1965 and demolished, and a new one erected on the same site in 1967. The station closed in February 2001; it is hoped that it will reopen in 2003 after a £1.7million refurbishment. *Inset*: the Finchley Constabulary along with members of the Boy Scouts are assembled at the rear of the station, *c.* 1915. Scouts were used to warn residents of imminent air attacks during the First World War.

Ballards Lane, *c.* 1920, showing the corner of Essex Park and the Wesleyan Chapel built in 1879. *Below*: the building is now the Finchley Methodist Church.

3
North Finchley

W. Collins and Sons' dairy cart, *c.* 1905. Collins had an outlet at 28 High Street, North Finchley, and a shop at 4 The Broadway, Regents Park Road.

A Metropolitan Electric Tramways repair vehicle at the tram sheds off Woodberry Grove. Trams operated along Ballards Lane and Regents Park Road to Golders Green from 16 December 1909 until they were replaced by the trolley buses on 2 August 1936. The sheds were later used for buses and the building is now a Homebase store.

High Road near the junction with Eton Avenue, *c.* 1930. Below in 2002: still a thriving shopping parade.

High Road looking towards Woodhouse Road, *c.* 1912. The corner was being developed at this time; note the advertising hoardings to the right of the tram.

High Road at the crossroads with Woodhouse Road, *c.* 1940. The National Provincial Bank is now a bar called Sea Rock. On the left is the Gaumont cinema. This is now a large building site (see below).

The Gaumont cinema. This building opened on 19 July 1937 and was built as a replacement for the Grand Hall across the road. It was a magnificent building designed by the architect W. Trent and had 2,000 seats, a café restaurant and a Compton organ. The organ was removed in 1967 to the Plough public house in Great Munden, Hertfordshire. The Gaumont closed on 25 October 1980 with the final film shown being aptly named *The Last Picture Show*. The land is now a large building site with plans for apartments an art centre and shopping (see artist's impression). *Top left*: the exterior, *c.* 1937. *Bottom left*: the entrance hall, *c.* 1937. *Above*: the cafeteria, *c.* 1937.

Nether Street, with Regent Close on the right and Trinity church on the left, *c.* 1930. This view is taken from an old picture postcard which had been wrongly captioned as Ballards Lane.

Nether Street looking towards the High Road with Trinity church on the right, *c*. 1910. The foundation stone was laid on 23 June 1864.

Regents Parade looking towards the Tally Ho, with Nether Street on the left, *c. 1930. Below*: the scene today.

The North Finchley tram terminus, *c.* 1936. Three different types of tram can be seen. This photograph was taken before the change-over to trolley buses. This was – until the current building works on the Gaumont site – still used as a bus terminus. The advertising hoardings around the land to the left will be familiar to Finchley residents as they have been in place since the demolition of the Gaumont.

High Road, *c.* 1914. The Grand Hall cinema, which closed in 1939, is seen on the right. *Inset*: a later view of the Grand Hall from the 1930s. *Below*: the view today. The large department store, once occupied by Owen Owen, is now shared by Argos and B'Wise.

Woodhouse Road *c.* 1910. Two sharply contrasting views of rural Finchley with a tram coming up the hill to the Tally Ho and today's busy junction with Summers Lane where a modern bus is using the same route.

The Cricketers Public House on the High Road opposite the Grand Hall, *c.* 1912. The pub is now called the Cherry Tree, as seen below.

Kingsway, *c.* 1933. A Feltham tram passing behind the Gaumont with Woodhouse Road in the background. *Below*: the modern equivalent, a no. 263 bus.

St Alban's Catholic church, *c.* 1930 and today. This is the corner of Birkbeck Road and Nether Street.

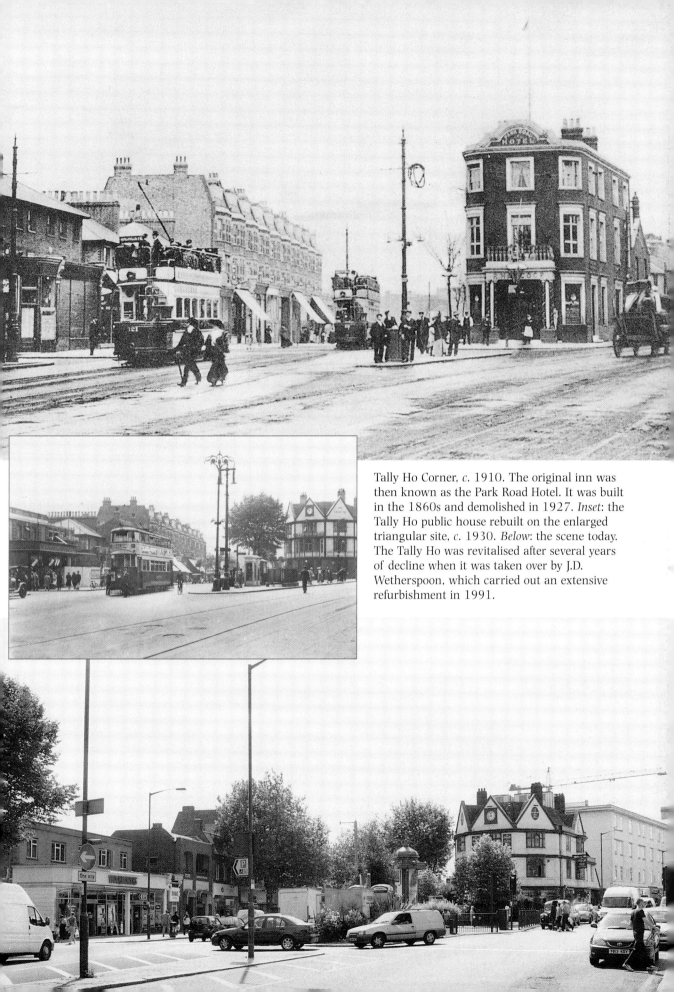

Tally Ho Corner, *c.* 1910. The original inn was then known as the Park Road Hotel. It was built in the 1860s and demolished in 1927. *Inset*: the Tally Ho public house rebuilt on the enlarged triangular site, *c.* 1930. *Below*: the scene today. The Tally Ho was revitalised after several years of decline when it was taken over by J.D. Wetherspoon, which carried out an extensive refurbishment in 1991.

High Street, looking towards the Tally Ho, *c.* 1920. The old Park Road Hotel can be seen behind the tramcar. On the left Priors old shop can be seen.

High Street, *c.* 1925. Priors department store was built in the early 1930s. It had three sales floors and was the first store in Finchley to have a passenger lift for customers. This building was destroyed by an oil bomb during the Second World War. *Below*: the High Street today is still a busy parade with several major retailers, including W. H. Smith.

Finchley Carnival, 27 June 1907. These floats are approaching the Tally Ho from the north. The carnival was in its centenary year in 2002. It was started to raise funds for charitable purposes including the building of the Finchley Cottage Hospital. *Below*: Carnival 2002 – a float has been decorated to celebrate Her Majesty Queen Elizabeth's Golden Jubilee. (*Photo by John Macdonald-Fulton*).

The Torrington Arms Hotel, on the corner of Lodge Lane, *c.* 1900. *Below*: in its current form, having been rebuilt in the early 1960s, now simply The Torrington, it is well known as a venue for live music.

High Street, *c.* 1930. The Torrington Hotel is on the left. The buildings are familiar but the traffic belongs to another age.

High Street, looking south, *c.* 1935. The Torrington Hotel is on the right.

High Street looking south with the dairy building on the right, *c.* 1920.

High Road looking north, *c.* 1912. On the left is the Finchley branch of the Manor Farm Dairy. The Sainsbury's store is on the right of the current picture. *Inset*: an early Sainsbury's delivery tricycle dressed up for the carnival, *c.* 1918.

High Road, *c.* 1912. Venner's butcher's shop at what was 96 High Road. *Right*: now 843 High Road, these premises are now occupied by the Hebah Indian restaurant.

Woodside Park Road looking towards the High Road, *c.* 1905. An Edwardian lady is cycling down the middle of the road towards the station. *Below*: the scene today with the inevitable parked cars.

Woodside Park station, *c.* 1905. The Great Northern Railway opened this station as Torrington Park, Woodside, on 1 April 1872. It was renamed Woodside Park on 1 May 1882.

Woodside Park station, *c.* 1910. London Transport Underground Northern Line trains began using Woodside Park station on 14 April 1940. *Below*: the major change today is the addition of a housing development on the extreme right.

The shops, Woodside Park Garden Suburb, *c.* 1940. It is now known as the Sussex Ring: see below.

High Road. The Odeon cinema, built by Starkey and Son, opened on 14 October 1935. It had 1,200 seats and lasted only 30 years, closing on 26 December 1964. It was converted into a garage and showrooms for Halls of Finchley. Today it is occupied by Furnitureland.

The Swan and Pyramids Public House, High
Road, *c.* 1905. *Inset*; a motor bus is parked
outside the pub, *c.* 1905.

Finchley Skating Rink opened in 1905. An extravagantly designed building, it was situated next to the Swan and Pyramids. In 1912 it became the Finchley Rink cinema with a resident concert party. It closed about 1915. *Inset*: managing directors and staff of the Skating Rink, *c*. 1905. *Below*: the starkly contrasting view today with the high brick wall of the Metropolitan Police garage, built in 1970.

Friern Watch Avenue, *c.* 1905. This typical Edwardian scene with unmade roads contrasts with today's view below and the heavy street parking.

Finchley Park, *c.* 1908. This is another side road which retains its original character but suffers from the usual clutter of parked cars.

Ravensdale Avenue, *c.* 1908. Note the unmade road and pavement for this side road off the High Road. Now near the entrance to Sainsbury's car park, it is a busy road with parking restrictions.

4

East Finchley

A large Hog Market was established here in the early nineteenth century.
The market was held in front of the old George Inn.

Manor Cottage Tavern, at the junction of East End Road and Green Lane, *c.* 1912. On the right are the railings of the St Marylebone Cemetery. The North Circular road, built in the 1920s, split East End Road just to the left of the pub. *Inset*: Manor Cottage Tavern, *c.* 1930. *Below*: today a recently finished completed housing development stands in the place of the old pub. The North Circular road goes under East End Road, replacing the roundabout.

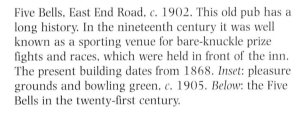

Five Bells, East End Road, *c.* 1902. This old pub has a long history. In the nineteenth century it was well known as a sporting venue for bare-knuckle prize fights and races, which were held in front of the inn. The present building dates from 1868. *Inset*: pleasure grounds and bowling green, *c.* 1905. *Below*: the Five Bells in the twenty-first century.

High Road, East Finchley, showing
the White Lion public house and the
railway bridge for the Great
Northern Railway, *c.* 1906.
Inset: building work as the present
White Lion is constructed.

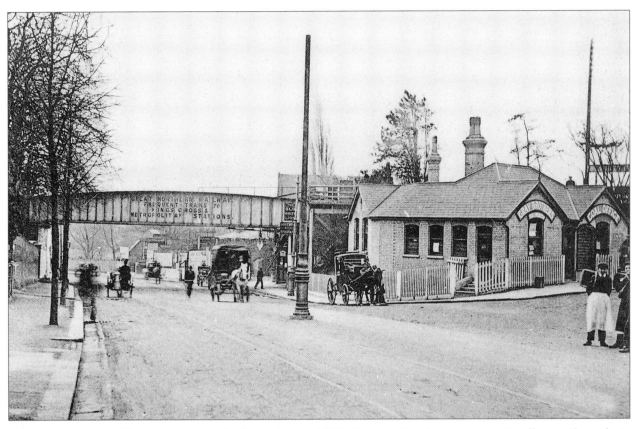

High Road, East Finchley, looking towards the station, *c.* 1905. Gray Brothers' coal merchant's office on the right is now part of the ticket office for the Underground.

East Finchley Great Northern Railway station, *c.* 1910. *Below*: the Northern Line station, 2002. This building dates from the late 1930s.

High Road from under the railway bridge looking north, *c.* 1906. *Below*: Today the building in the centre is the head office of McDonald's Restaurants Ltd.

High Road at the junction with Fairlawn Avenue. The Picturedrome, opened in 1910, was soon renamed the Coliseum. It was refurbished in the late 1930s and renamed the Rex, and in November 1975 it resurfaced as the Phoenix. *Below*: the cinema in 2002. It is now one of the oldest surviving cinemas in the country.

The Bald Faced Stag, *c.* 1890. East Finchley Congregational church can be seen on the right. *Below*: the scene today. The church was demolished in 1965.

High Road near the junction with Lincoln Road, *c.* 1908. *Inset*: an advertisement from W.A. Hanchet and Co., cemetery masons. *Below*: the High Road in 2002 with the Local Café on the corner.

Grove Parade, *c.* 1914. The parade was part of the High Road at the junction with Squires Lane. The nearest building, no. 18, was the Squires Lane post office, but this building has now been demolished.

Lewis Gardens, *c.* 1920. A cyclist is resting his bike on the kerb. *Below*: the view today blighted by parked cars and graffiti.

5

Whetstone

The Blue Anchor public house, *c.* 1910. The picture shows Miss Jessie Ferry, landlady, outside the pub, which was situated in the High Road.

High Road, Whetstone, *c.* 1925. On the left is the Swan with Two Necks public house, demolished in 1960. The advertising board is for the Birley Road estate off Totteridge Lane, and is offering new houses with a garage space for £795. *Below*: the scene in 2002. The shops and offices on the right are still the same and the street sign for Swan Lane recalls the old pub which stood there.

High Street, Whetstone, *c.* 1940. Motor-buses were running at the same time as the trolley-buses; on the right is the Griffin public house. The scene today shows a busy junction with the Griffin still serving ale.

High Road, Whetstone, looking towards Finchley with the Griffin on the left, *c.* 1945. In the centre of the picture stands the old pub, the Hand and Flower, which along with a row of houses was demolished and is now Barclays Bank, as seen below.

High Road, Whetstone, *c.* 1910. This view shows the corner of Totteridge Lane. The corner has recently been redeveloped and Boots the Chemist now have a large store here.

High Road, *c.* 1910. The Bull and Butcher public house is on the left. Virtually all of the parade has now been demolished and replaced by shops with flats above.

High Road, *c*. 1910. In the centre is the Green Man public house, which was rebuilt in 1890. The building is still intact: it is now the Green Man Tyre and Exhaust centre.

High Road looking north, *c. 1920. Below:* the same view today, once again a mixture of old and new.

High Road, Whetstone,
c. 1920. Next to the
Bull public house stood
the Palace Hotel, which
was demolished in the
1930s and replaced by
shops and flats.

The Three Horseshoes, High Road, Whetstone, with Friern Barnet Lane to the left of the pub, 1905 and today.

6

Friern Barnet

Colney Hatch Lane, *c.* 1905. The parish of Friern Barnet, which included the hamlet of
Colney Hatch, had a population of 2,330 in 1871.

The Orange Tree, Friern Lane, *c.* 1905. There has been a public house on this site since the sixteenth century. *Below:* the Orange Tree in the twenty-first century.

Friern Barnet Road at the junction with Station Road, *c.* 1905. On the left stands the Turrets public house (see inset), and on the right the bank has now been converted into a public house named appropriately the Bankers Draft.

Colney Hatch Hospital was originally known as Middlesex County Lunatic Asylum. This large building covered an area of 25 acres. It had accommodation for over 2,000 patients. The first stone was laid by Prince Albert in 1849. It was opened on 17 July 1851, and the architect was Mr S.W. Daukes. The building was set in grounds of approximately 100 acres. In later years the hospital became Friern Mental Hospital then the Friern Hospital, and finally closed in 1993. It has in recent years been converted into luxury apartments.

ACKNOWLEDGEMENTS & PICTURE CREDITS

F*inchley Past and Present* has been a pleasure to complete. While the majority of the pictures are from the Memories Picture Library we have had some assistance, and special thanks go to Nicky Hillman, Tony Moss, Neal Garner, Nick Benn, John Whittington and Rod Brewster and Peter Beal at the *Hendon and Finchley Times*.

The Memories collection started in the 1960s, when Clive Smith started collecting postcards of Hendon. In 1973 Clive published his first book, *Hendon As It Was*. This in turn created a demand in the area for pictures from the book and also more interest in local history. 1975 saw the publication of *Finchley As It Was*. In 1979 the Hendon Collectors Centre was opened in Greyhound Hill where Clive sold postcards, books and reproductions from the collection. In 1981 the collection moved to a Bell Lane shop, where Clive and David continued publishing local books and selling pictures of the local area.

Memories Picture Library is now at 130/132 Brent Street, a large double-fronted shop on the main road in Hendon. Pictures, framing and old picture postcards are available. Clive's eldest son, David, who produces the photographic reproductions for the collection, has taken all the modern pictures for this book. Clive and David both started their careers in Fleet Street, Clive working in the library and David in the darkroom. They now work together at Memories collecting more pictures and preserving our local history.

Copies of the pictures from this book and all our publications are available from:
Memories Picture Library, 130/132 Brent Street, Hendon, London NW4 2DR
Tel 020 8203 1500 Fax 020 8203 7031
www.memoriespostcards.co.uk